Title

Success Mastery Education: Success Habits for Peak Performance in Life and Work

Benjamin S C Ugoji

Contents

Introduction

"Success is to be measured not so much by the position that one has reached in life as by the obstacles which he has overcome." *Booker T. Washington*

The word *"success"* each time it is mentioned, resonates or brings to light different images in the mind of individuals. Love it or loath it there is deep down within us – human beings the desire to be successful rather than to be failures.

I want to be successful in life and I bet that is the desire for you who is reading this book. Why should I really bother about been successful? My simple answer to this question is that deep within our human nature is the urge to do well. However, most of the time; this is not achievable because we lack the important ingredient in terms of our ability and capacity to seize the opportunities before us.

If God created us in His image and after His likeness; it does seems to me that He has impacted us with all the abilities to succeed. Moreover, the most important remit that God gave us in our sojourn here on earth is to increase, multiply, replenish and subdue the earth. And we are His workmanship in Christ Jesus and His purpose is that we do good works in this life.

I am an inquisitive person, and this may have fuelled my passion to be a continuous learner. What is it that makes some people to succeed where others have failed? What is this essential ingredient that is common to those men that are deemed successful?

First these great people are men of thought, who through great effort of action have organised their ideas to results that fulfil their ideals.

According to Edison, genius is 1% inspiration and 99% perspiration. Earl Prevette had this to say: Geniuses are only people who keep busy in their perfection of a science or an art.

"The heights by great men reached and kept were not attended by sudden flight. But they, while their companion slept were toiling upward in the night."

I do not present myself to be successful in all areas of my life. But if that is my purpose and this work is testament to my desire to move in this direction then I am being successful. However, I have been endowed with the ability to observe, think, organise and act with information and what I have discovered are shared with you in this book.

I sincerely welcome you aboard of this journey, which in diverse ways will shape your character and destiny towards great achievement.

This book has been divided into four parts as you can see from the content. Each part is made of topics and these topics ends with activities to help you challenge your status quo and propel you to move out of your comfort zone.

Success is action. It does not come by chance but it is a choice that you make today for a better tomorrow. I leave you with this question. How do you want your life to play out in the next five years; a life of mediocre or excellence?

 You decide!

I hope you will enjoy as well as put the lessons into practice so as to develop mastery in your success journey.

"Success is doing – not wishing!
Frances Coombes - Author of Self Motivation

Part 1 – Success and You

"Success comes only to the man who acts most effectively on what he knows."
-Norval A Hawkins

Success means different things to people. For one thing it is an individual journey a person sets out towards an accomplishment.

In this section the meaning of success as seen from different authors is reviewed. Success should be seen as a personal responsibility and each person is encouraged to persevere towards making his /her dream come true. At the end of this section is an activity which challenges you to answer the questions so as to check your own understanding.

It is important that you answer the questions at the end of each chapter; if you desire to make progress.

1
Success an overview

"Success comes to those who become success conscious. Failure comes to those who indifferently allow themselves to become failure conscious."
Napoleon Hill
Best Selling Author- Think and Grow Rich

There is always an outcome to each habit or behaviour that we exhibit. Most of them lead to successful outcome. But some are not palatable because they led to failure. It's important that we need to be clear the result or outcome that we desire in any endeavour so that we can measure or control the nature of our progress. The ability for us to achieve success depends on our internal as well as our external reference systems or the way we think, feel, and act towards a given situation.

These depend on first and foremost the way we think about ourselves. This has to do with our confidence to effectively take the challenge and to complete it. For example, if it's an experience that we are familiar with we have the confidence that we can efficiently tackle the situation because of our repertoire of skills, experience, knowledge and resources. Therefore we're able to put all the effort required to achieve our outcome. These require the development of our thoughts, managing our emotion which imparts on our mood and attitude and taking effective action.

What is success? According to John C Maxwell, Leadership Expert and Best Selling Author: "Success is: knowing your purpose in life, growing to reach your maximum potential, and sowing seeds that benefit others."

From Maxwell's definition, success is a journey. It starts with determining your life's purpose and doing all you can to maximise your potential – growth and contribution, and sowing the seeds that benefits others. This is the path to blessing.

Glenn Bland the author of Success! The Glenn Bland Method is of the opinion that true success avoids extremes. It is a journey and also a gradual process. He reasoned that success abides in the realm where balanced living is achieved. According to Glenn, balanced living result in happiness and success; for our Creator intends for us to lead happy and successful lives by applying the natural laws established by him to keep us in tune with the universe.

The three attributes of success from Glenn point of view are:

1. Direction – setting your sights on things that are worthwhile in life and then establishing a plan to continuously work towards their fulfilment and accomplishment.
2. Balance – keeping proper perspective about every area of your life. Staying in harmony with nature's law which produces perfect balance. Balance in all things brings about happiness.
3. Belief – no one can become successful who does not possess belief. The greater the belief the greater the degree of success. Successful men are believer!

From Glenn Bland point of view:

"Success is the progressive realisation of predetermined, worthwhile goals, established with balance and purified by belief."

According to David McNally in his book: "*Even the eagles need a Push*" proposed that each of us will define and measure success differently. Some will place more emphasis on the economic score then others. However, no matter your choice, if you want to succeed, you must understand that your rewards in life will be in direct proportion to the contribution you make. The principle of contribution stipulates that rewards - follow service, getting follow - giving, and making an impression - follow making a difference. In other words, before determining what you want, you need to clarify what it is you have to offer.

If you gasp this fundamental principle, apply it to your work and you'll have little concern for money again. Apply it to your personal and professional relationships, and you'll be overwhelmed with love, adventure and respect you receive from others.

Your success depends upon:

- The things you choose to focus on in life
- The meaning or interpretation you put upon the information you receive
- The action you take as a result of processing that information

Three attributes namely your perception, process and performance with regards to how you attend to information and experience are pivotal to your being successful or not. This involves the realms of your thought, feelings and actions which results in your life's experience. It encompasses vision, thought and action in a desired direction towards your destiny.

Let's look at the principles prescribed by God to Joshua the son of Nun after the death of Moses in the Book of Joshua:

"Never stop reading this Scroll of the Law. Day and night you must think about what it says. Make sure you do everything that is written in it. Then things will go well with you. And you will have great success (Joshua 1:7)."

"Here is what I am commanding you to do. Be strong and brave. Do not be terrified. Do not loose heart. I am the LORD your God. I will be with you everywhere you go (Joshua 1:8)."

For me this is the fundamental doctrine for success. To pursue success without the wisdom of God is disaster. God is the author of wisdom and knowledge for a successful life. God has a purpose for your life, he has a goal and plan and he wants you to trust in His counsel and depend on Him.

Your success is the product of unconscious beliefs and feelings. To become successful in any area of life, you must identify and clear the unconscious blocks that are holding you back.

This is summarised succinctly by Fritz Perls in the following words:

"It's awareness ... of how you are stuck, that make you recover."

Jim Rohn - the American Foremost Business Philosopher had this to say:

"Success is not to be pursued; it is to be attracted by you person you become."

This is the fundamental for success doctrine – you change your being, which changes what you do and therefore the result you get.

Goals and plans are principles to happiness and success. This is because they help us to create abundance as well as help to give meaning, purpose, hope and pleasure to life. The statistics has it that 3% of the population have their goals and plan written down, 10% have their goals and plan in their head , not written down, The rest 67% drift through life without definite goals or plans and they do not know where they are going and others dictate to them.

It was revealed that 3% who have goals and plans written down are 50 – 100% more successful than the 19% who have their goal and plans in their head.

The main of this work is to motivate you the reader to achieve more in life through having direction by way of having a purpose and setting and establishing concrete practical plans to making to our dream a reality.

In the book of proverbs we hear this admonition:

"The wisdom of the prudent is to understand his way: but the folly of fools is deceit."

Proverbs 14;8

David MacNelly reasoned that success begins the moment we understand that life is about growing: it is about acquiring the knowledge and skills we need to move more fully and effectively.

If you become determined and committed to walk in this path of success, you'll not be afraid to fail, take risk, rejected or be alone based on your dream to fulfil your dream. According to Frederick Wilcox:

"Progress always involves risk; you can't steal second base and keep your foot on the first."

In his book Lead the Field, Earl Nightingale said that:
Success requires the conscious utilization of ourselves in the service of others. We can become whatever we seriously make up our minds to become. Whatever we seriously decide to do is naturally linked to our genetic possibilities. Just pursue your natural aptitude.

Anyone who is on course towards a worthy goal is successful. Success does not lie in the achievement of a goal but in its pursuit. Success is a journey!

What habits or traits separate super successful people from dreamers?

"The man of success is the man possessed of the greatest spiritual understanding and every great fortune comes from superior and truly superior power." Prentice Mullford

This is not an easy question. But there are attributes, strategies, techniques or belief systems exhibited by successful people in their different fields throughout the ages. I have tried to research and read through some of the ideas presented by different individuals. There is common thread visible in the behavioural traits of successful people in the way they deal with themselves, other people and the result they deliver in their different activities. The main thing is that super successful people have developed mastery in their particular endeavours and have in turn become great leaders rather than followers. They have learnt to serve other people through the solution that they bring to the market place.

The following are some of the attributes of displayed by successful people:

1. **Good thinker** – Most successful people are first and foremost great thinkers. They have the ability to think through their problems and to figure out the solution to their problems. They have the ability to engage the expertise of those who will help them to follow through.

2. **Visionaries – decide on their dreams and goals -** Successful people see and imagines in their minds eyes what they want. They set goals with clear objectives; and plans on how to accomplish them. Moreover they motivated and move forward towards the accomplishments of their vision.

3. **Strong self-belief** – On the average successful people believe that they are the one that are responsible for their success. They have strong believe in

their ability and capacity to achieve their goal that they move on with confidence even when others do not believe in their dream. They progress steadily towards the realisation of their goals.

4. **Passionate and enthusiastic** – successful people are very passionate about the purpose for which they are engaged in. Most of the time the tenacity with which they tackle their dream robs on others because of their great enthusiasm. This is likely what MJ Demarco, the author of "The Millionaire Fastlane" referred to as PULL and PUSH for success. In PULL for success the successful person sets the ball rolling whereas in PUSH for success you are waiting for someone to ignite the fire of your fireplace in order for you to succeed. An example of pull for success is "where you write your own book and self- publish it; then publishers call you"; as opposed to PUSH for success; "where you send your manuscript to a publisher."

5. **Extraordinarily creative** – Creativity is the ability is see old thing s in new ways. Creative people are able to see patterns that could results in new innovations. On the whole most successful people writers, poets, scientists, business men, financiers, teachers, etc have realised how to use creative imagination and constructive imagination to reap abundance in their chosen field. In the case of applying their creative imagination they have learnt to idealise, visualise and materialise their dreams. And they use apply the skill of constructive imagination to figure out what they want and set plans to attain their dream. It is apt to say they are always on the lookout for new ways of doing things - literally, thinking out of the box.

6. **Take action (action takers not action fakers)** – Without action no idea or dream will be idealised. Successful people understand this and they do all

that they can through manipulating their environment by taking action. As always, action trumps inaction and wherever there is constructive action towards an endeavour; the results shows.

7. **Lifelong learner/continuous improvers -** No matter their filed of endeavour, successful people realise that for them to up their game they must be lifelong learners. They also understand that they need to continually improve themselves so as to be able to face their competition and deliver excellent value for their clients.

8. **Never give up – commitment, persistent and determined -** Successful people do not reply on reason why they will not achieve but rather they focus on the result. They never give up and will always try to figure out or revise the means, plan, strategy and tactics to reach their goal. They are very focused and committed to the task at hand and persistently move forward to conquer new grounds; if need be.

9. **Excel in what they do best –** Successful people desire to achieve as well as excel in their different fields. They realise that competence and excellence can only be realised through practice; therefore they constantly strive to make good progress so as to break new grounds in their chosen fields. They have also come to the realisation that what they need is outside their comfort zone and they give what it takes in order to get what they want.

10. **Focus on resources (time, money, effort) –** Whatever you focuses on increases. If you focus on lack of resources this what you will see. However, successful people have the ability to identify and focus on the available resources and use it to implement their desires.

11. **Game changers – innovative, different –** most successful people tend to think differently that their counterparts. They think about solution to problems and hence are constantly looking for new ways to add value to best serve the society. They are not afraid to be different and for most part are the pioneers that drive innovation forward in their chosen career.

12. **Integrity – true to themselves and responsible –** Successful people seek to serve people with the best of their talent and abilities. They are very honest and genuine about their estimation of themselves and are always willing to give their best.

13. **Right attitude –** Having the right emotional landscape is the main thing in any business. And successful people from all works of life have it. The right attitude will not take the place of other important skills set required to any successful outcome, but it determines how far you will go. Remember, that your attitude determines your altitude. They have the can do attitude and will always fine turn their attitudes to suit the job at hand.

14. **Risk takers – unafraid of the unknown –** Successful people are risk takers. They move ahead of their dream but would compensate from the risk through application of special knowledge in their chosen field that helps them to minimise risk. The chose to use their power of the knowledge that that their success is outside of their comfort zone and therefore move forward progressively through small steps.

15. **Good networkers / communicators –** Most successful people have learnt the importance of networking and linking up with like mind or their clients alike. They have come to understand that developing rapport within their audience groups is key to their thriving in their respective domains.

16. **Great leaders** – Successful people, more often than not are leaders in their chosen fields or careers. They have the desire to give of their skills, knowledge, experience and aptitude in their different fields of endeavour. In turn they draw a lot of followers as a result.

17. **Good planners – with good organisational skills and execute second to none** – Most successful people know that that in order to achieve their desire they need to create a plan. The also devise means to work on their plan so as to achieve their dream. Most successful people have learnt to put their desires into a plan and take action to making it a reality.

18. **Extremely successful people live in the present moment** – Successful people live in the Now. They know that it is in the present moment that they can do what they do. For them the past is gone and the future is uncertain, but they constantly strive to make the best of their present moment. This is because they have realised that time is of great essence and that their ability can only serve in the now.

19. **They are usually relaxed and keep their perspective** – successful people have learnt to choose emotions that support the goal that they pursue. They are courageous and confident in the tasks ahead and pursue it with vital vigour. In any given environment, they are able to see what others cannot see. They have trained their senses to see opportunities in uncommon places.

20. **Successful People have an inquisitive nature – always asking questions** Asking positive question that support effective mental attitude and cisposition is very productive. Successful people have mastered the ability to ask question that help to challenge their limiting belief. This helps them to fight against obstacle on their way to reaching their dreams from negative thinking, negative feeling and obstacles on their physical environment.

21. **Successful People have master mind groups** – successful people have master mind groups where they learn from each other. It is a case of iron sharpening iron and a man been sharpened by the countenance of his friends. They share the special knowledge of the belief, values, strategies and tactics that led to their success to those in their groups that would want to learn. This idea is seen in the activities in the networking sites in the internet – like the *Facebook, Twitter, LinkedIn, E-academy* to mention but few where people have forums of people they follow.

22. **Successful People respect the value of the contribution they make** – First and foremost successful believe that that the ideas thst they bring to the marketplace are valuable. They set process in place to bring these ideas in form of products, services, and websites to the audience that they serve. The have the ability to sell these ideas and to profit from them.

23. **Successful People are masters of empathy, rather than sympathy** – Successful people are not selfish. They are able to empathise with other people's needs and take action in positive ways as to meet such needs. They have the emotional intelligence to think in terms of the other person and are passionate about helping them actualise their dreams.

24. **Successful people practice the fundamentals and master the mundane** Successful people understand that the big tasks are small tasks put together. And that some of the basic fundamentals to great achievements are: *be prepared, be present and be on time.* Therefore the saying by Robin Sharma that: "ability to perform the basics paves the way to develop and perform at a higher level of mastery"; is correct. Remember that success is a journey and along the way, many tasks will be exciting or mundane but a successful

person never ponders, they are steadfast in all of it through and through. The art of doing the mundane separates success from failure. In any area of life how successful you become could be in your willingness to roll up your sleeves and help with anything. The idea here is that success is built moment by moment. In an article written on The Foundation of Foundation of Success – the mundane, (http://performance-advantage.net) Dennis R Buckley said that:

"If you take the time to study the truly successful people in the world you will find that each one of them toiled in obscurity for years and then became an overnight success. You see while they were unknown they were working on themselves in the mundane, forming the foundation of their success through study, learning, implementing, failing, fixing, sacrifice, and trying and trying again until it worked"

25. Successful people do what unsuccessful people are NOT willing to do

Successful people generally do what successful people are willing to do. They are able to see opportunities in uncertain places and transform the opportunities to ideas, services, products or merchandise to meet peoples' needs. And as a result, they contribute their skills, talents, knowledge and resources to make their dream come true. This idea is fundamental to most great act of success in diverse fields.

26. Successful people are flexible and tolerable

Successful people have realised through their experience and way of thinking that the map is not the territory. Therefore they are always ready to make a detour in their original plan, strategy and tactics towards the realisation of their dream. They know that the plan is not written in stone but can be revised as the need arises.

27. Efficient time management

Successful people are productive with time. The end up creating intangible to tangible evidence of their use of time which can in turn be translated into great value. They realise that time is now and use their abilities and capacity in the present to intelligently leverage time to their advantage.

Activity 1: Success an overview

1. Write your own definition of success:

2. Mention one area you need to succeed.

3. What can you need to do today to pull the success that you need above a reality?

4. Study the biography of a successful person in any field. Review their attributes in terms of those listed of successful people.

5. Which of these attributes do you need to cultivate?

2

Good thinking is the basis for all progress and success

"All progress and success springs from thinking."

Edison

Before exploring this topic further, it's important give a brief description of what thinking is all about. Thinking is the mental manipulation of information stored in form of concepts, images or proposition. The ability to think frees us from the confines of immediate present. In his book on thinking course, Edward De Bono, had this to say about thinking:

"Thinking is the operating skill through which intelligence acts upon experience."

In the book he mentioned that intelligence is a potential; and, thinking is an operating skill. Therefore this preamble is clear on the link between intelligence, thinking and experience.

A lot has been written concerning thinking, success and making progress in life and the conclusion is that:

Successful people think differently than unsuccessful people

Thinking is a skill that has to be learned, developed and mastered. The reason that most people don't realise it is that they are not aware and moreover, thinking is not easy.

"Thinking is hard work, and that is why few do it."

Albert Einstein

But like any other skill if you put your heart to it you'll master it and the reward is tremendous in terms of you being able to achieve your potential and make progress in life.

"You are today where your thoughts have brought you. You will be tomorrow where your thoughts take you."

James Allen

Your thought is your blueprint for success

Every experience you'll ever have begins in your mind. Most people look outside of themselves to get inspiration as to what they can achieve or not achieve. Your whole life experience for the future is locked in your imagination. You can unlock this potential through changing your mind or rather the way you think. Whatever you do; you still have to belief in being to able bring this trains of thought of possibilities locked in your imagination to fruition. Our thinking is to be based on value.

"Whatever things are true . . . noble . . . just . . . pure . . . lovely . . . are of good report, if there is any virtue and if thee is anything praiseworthy, think on these things."

- **Paul the Apostle**

The values of your thoughts process will ultimately determine your destiny and therefore your legacy in life. It is a choice you make daily.

If you have the freedom to nurture good thoughts wouldn't it be rewarding in the long run if you make it a habit?

The key to becoming a success is to develop the thinking habit of successful people. It's important to realise that your character, your thinking, and your beliefs are a critical part of want determines the level of your success.

Success is thinking in action

"... A lot of people know what to do, but few actually do what they know, knowing is not enough! You must take action."

- **Anthony Robbins – Author of Unlimited Power**

Imagine that you thought of planting a seed in your garden and never had a practical plan of action to actually execute it. What will such a mental activity profit you without a corresponding and effective action for its accomplishment? Most people look at success in one level where there are two sides to it: the mental (thinking) and the physical (action). The former takes place in our head but later in our immediate environment. According to one coach:

"Mental is to physical what four is to one."

Taking action is the manipulation of the physical environment so as to make our idea a reality.

To make progress in any filed you have to take action. But the success of the action you take depends entirely on how you think beforehand.

"The successful people in industry have succeeded through their thinking. Their hands were helpers to their brain."

- **Claude M Bristol – Author of the Magic of Believing**

Therefore success is thinking and doing!

Create your blueprint for success – craft your TFA script®"
The beginning of a habit is like an invisible tread, but overtime we repeat the act we strengthen the strand, and add to it another filament, until it becomes a great cable and bind it irrevocably, thought and action."
Orison Swett Marden

The TFA script is my own acronym which I created to amplify the fact that we write

our own story be it a success or failure based on our thoughts, feelings and actions.

It seems as a very bold statement but experience shows that we can change our

outcome by changing the way we do any three of these.

One of the greatest advices we'll ever have on the working of the human mind is that

Paul the Apostle gave in the book of Romans 12:2

". . . Be transformed by the renewing of your mind . . . "

The key ideas here are:

- You can be transformed
- Your mind can be renewed

Hence transformation comes from the renewing of your mind. The result of this

transformation leads to increased awareness of Divine purpose.

Therefore, you can change your mind so as to change your life. How is this

possible?

Remember that your thinking has to be based on value. In our waking day we do

three things: we think, feel and act and these impact on the results we get.

The idea of TFA script is that we can choose to nurse those thoughts, feelings and action that empower so as to create the results we desire. It is a learning and change process that requires dedication and commitment on our part.

Thought leads to feelings.

Feelings leads to action.

Actions leads to results.

The basis for creating this TFA script is based on the understanding that we create the results we have based on our thinking, feelings and actions.

We need to become aware and responsible for our thoughts and actions. Taking action is thinking in motion which is a cause and effect relationship that sets particular cause in motion leading to a resultant effect with time.

Change your thinking to change your life
"As a man thinketh in his heart so he is."
Proverbs 23:7

I read an interesting story attributed to an explorer by Earl Prevette in his book: "How to turn your ability into cash" The explorer was asked what exploration he enjoyed most. His answer was for him to sit in an old – fashioned rocking chair and exploring the undiscovered regions inside his own mind. In exploring the undiscovered regions inside the mind man discovers that he has interest His interest creates desire. Desires are of two natures: one is physical and the other mental. Each of these desire requires channels of expression. Subsistence and propagation satisfy the physical and thoughts and ideas satisfy the mental desire.

"Ability is the positive thoughts on the job to deliver to you the things you desire,"
- **Earl Prevette**

If you want to move to the next level in the ladder of life, you need to become more effective in the way you think and act. Good thinking lead to confident and competent performance and therefore to better rewards from life. Well, you'll say to me how is it so? Just look around you, among the successful people you come across in life. They have the knack of being able to think differently. They think about abundance when others are thinking about scarcity, solution rather than problem, how to contribute rather than what to get, leading rather than needing, and possibility rather than impossibility. They believe that they are the one able to bring the change they need by first of all changing themselves to what they want to become. Therefore success is who you've become. You can learn to be successful in any endeavour if you commit yourself to it. For example, you can learn to create wealth, manage it and invest it. Most successful people went through a process of failure before they learned how to be successful in their areas of expertise.

If you change your thinking you change your belief and if you change your belief you change your expectation, and when you change your expectation you change your attitude, when you change your attitude your behaviour changes and when you change your behaviour your performance is changed and ultimately your life is changed. There is the need for you to be in a continuous flux of change and growth.

The key thing here is that when you want to move to the next level in life you have to raise your standard; change your limiting beliefs and change your capability.

In his book "Leading the Field", Earl Nightingale had this to say:

"Successful people are not people without problems. They are people who have learned to solve their problems by thinking. Thinking bridges the gap between our present point and our goals. 92% of our worries are useless. Of the remaining 8%, half pertain to problems we can't solve and half to those we can solve if we'll learn how.

Activity 2

Critically review the following steps in your thinking process:

Thought > Belief > Expectation> Attitude > Behaviour > Performance > Changed Life

Which areas do you need to focus on in the present condition or circumstance that you're facing so as to succeed?

3

Take responsibility of your life
"Experience is not what happens to a man, it is what a man does with what happens to him."
Aldous Huxley

What does being responsible mean to you? An answer to this question will begin to define what it is for one to be responsible for our life. Being responsible has to do with being in control of our thinking, feeling and behaviour. The word responsibility means, 'response-ability"; our ability to respond.

If you want to succeed in any given situation you have to understand that you'll be responsible to creating the experience. Being responsible is being aware of what goes on in your thinking, the pictures you paint in your mind (visualisation) and the action that you take or didn't take. In any event, the response that you take results in the outcome you receive.

Simply put:

$$E \quad + \quad R \quad = \quad O$$

If you want to change your outcome, you have to change the way you response to situations or life's experience.

Being responsible is a call to be proactive rather than reactive. It's a carefully thought out plan on the outcome you desire on being exposed to a Stimulus and our Response to it.

This is made possible through making use of four of Human Endowments namely described by Stephen Covey in his book: "7 habits of highly effective people."

1 Self-awareness – being self-aware has to do with how you response to different information that we perceive and process as well as the implication of those unconscious thoughts that impact the way we behave. It's like asking if we know how our thoughts process impact our behaviour and decision making skills and therefore the results we produce. Therefore we need to continually examine, our thoughts, moods and behaviour.

Awareness - is knowing what is happening around you. Self-awareness is knowing what you are experiencing

2 Imagination – imagination is visualising beyond experience and present reality. How can you unlock the benefits of resourceful ideas locked in your imagination? Most great creators and innovators rely on their imagination for their creative talents and abilities. Remember what Albert Einstein said that "imagination is greater than knowledge." Your imagination set in the future without past limitation and you can fan it into fame through practice by doing the following;

- Setting aside time alone away from interruption, and muse over the event or situation using the right brain

- Try and visualise a more positive and fruitful response.

3 Conscience – man's conscience is the candle of God searching through your hidden motive. Another apt description of conscience was a quote used by a local newspaper for its motto. It say:

"Conscience is an open wound and only truth will heal it."

Basically, it is means understanding right and wrong and following personal integrity. What is integrity? Well Earl Nightingale had this to say:

"Integrity is the seed for achievement. It is the principle that never fails. Integrity means completely fulfilling your own unique combination of powers. **Integrity is being all you can be, doing all you can do and having all you can have.** Integrity is wholeness, togetherness and completeness. There is no piece missing, nothing hidden."

Development of this attribute requires that you need to become more reflective in your thinking. You need to put the feedback into action – you must respond to the outcome. This ability will be lost if you become adamant in applying the truth: hence the phrases "sear your conscience as with hot iron."

4   Independent Will – this is acting independent of external influence. As God's creation we have the freedom and choice to make decision you will help us to use our God given talent to realise our potential and fulfil our destiny. Therefore the ability develop and use this endowment of independent will enable us to exercise imagination and conscience. A strong independent will according to Stephen Covey, allows you to act in a more powerful way than the forces around; enabling you to swim upstream.

Therefore each time you are faced with an outcome to an event in your life or a decision making process – learn to make use of these four human endowments which have been freely give to you. According to John Whitmore in his book: Coaching for performance - **"Awareness and Responsibility are without doubt two qualities that are crucial to performance in any activity."**

Activity 3: **Take responsibility of your life**

1. Which areas in your life do you need to be more responsible?

2. What do need to do so as to achieve this objective?

Part 2- Success Paths
"You must be before you can do or have something"
Earl Nightingale - Author lead the Field

People have different conception as per the road to success. Success is not to be

pursed it is who you have become. In his section the nuts and bolts in terms of the

cognitive stakes for being successful is progressively explored.

The mindset for success is a growing mindset rather than a fixed one. The other side

of the coin: failure is looked into as to find out its place in the success journey. On

the whole the various obstacles that will impinge on our being success are evaluated

and guidance given as how to use then as tools to accomplishing our desires.

4

Discover your life's purpose
You don't invent mission you detect it
Victor Franklin

There is no road to success but through a clear, strong purpose. A purpose underlies character, culture, position, attainment of whatever sort.
--T. T. MUNGER.

What is your purpose in life and how do you discover your purpose? A lot has been written about how to discover our life's purpose. But no matter what has been written we need to understand that deep down in our spirit man there is the yearning to perform a particular task or work to benefit others. Each of should feel differently to this very calling, but the main idea is that there is a reason for your being. What are you here to do? What is it that makes you thick? Throughout history great achievers and people of great accomplishment are men and women who have discovered their purpose. If you can remember anything - when we were created, God made us for a purpose. We are meant to increase, multiply, replenish and subdue the earth. All these paint a picture of growth and contribution. Therefore, we are supposed to be instruments of righteousness.

We are endowed with diverse gifts, talents, special knowledge and experience. How can we use these to serve our generation? To my mind your purpose is to discover these talents and how to best use them to serve humanity.

A lot has been written on this topic. But we'll try to explore more on this topic and how our understanding of it is important in our success journey.

What do you feel passionate about?

People who are on purpose are very passionate on what they do. They believe that that their activities add value to people's life while at the same time help them to make sense of their contribution. Passion is an indicator of what you value; it is what draws you, holds your attention keeps you thinking late at night. It could be that one thing that you could do if you have all the resources and money you need. What is it that you are naturally drawn to and would even do for nothing? This could be the clue to your purpose.

Purpose comes from knowing

According to Frances Coombes, purpose comes knowing that what you do align with your beliefs and values. Beliefs, values and purpose are our drivers – they motivate us and make us who we are. It's very simple. If you don't know what drives you, you cannot motivate yourself to be more effective or press your own triggers to get the results you want from life. It's important to further look at our values and beliefs.

Values
"Authentic values are those by which a life can be lived."
Allan Bloom

Values are things which are important to you. They are the ideals which you build your life around. According, to Michael Happel, author of - "How to be brilliant – change your life in 90 days." Values are up there with oxygen!

Values are the principles that drive our behaviour; they give meaning to our lives. When we engage with what we do with our values we engage in projects with our hearts (spirit) and minds. Our belief and values define who we are and what we do. They can be described as the personal rules which we choose to live by.

What is your core value? Your core value will affect what you say, what you think, and action you take. Values are what make us the way we are, they drive us and provide motivation for how we live our lives. When we know what our values are, we are aware of the behaviour that spring from holding these value, you are in a position to set clear goals and decisions about what's important to us and what we want in life. Values are the key to living a motivational, successful and rewarding life.

Do you know your values? If you do, are you living your life based on these values? Or are you living your life based on someone else's value?

Your values are what you build everything on, if your value system is right, if the belief system that you have is pushing you in the right direction, then you'll achieve all you ever need to.

Beliefs

According to John C Maxwell, in his book *"Thinking for Change"*, a belief is not just an idea you possess: it is an idea that possesses you.

Beliefs are different from values. Beliefs are locked in our thought system, since if we change our thought process, our beliefs is changed. You can beliefs things that are actually not true. We need to continually analyse and change our beliefs as new evidence that undermine our beliefs is received.

Since belief is very important in our ability to receive the things you desire, therefore, you need to guard your thought. The reason is that your belief is shaped to a large extent by the things you observe and think about. Hence it is important that you should command your attention.

How to develop and write your life purpose – an exercise

From the above preambles, we've looked at the basis for discovering your life's purpose. A lot has been written on how to write your life's purpose. But in this section we'll look at the example described by Jack Canfield in his book – "From where you are to where you want to be."

1. List two of your unique qualities, such as *enthusiasm and creativity*.

2. List one or two ways you enjoy expressing these qualities when interacting with others such as *to support or to inspire*.

3. Assume the world is a perfect right now. What does this world look like? How is everyone interacting with everyone else? What does it feel like? Write your answer in form of a statement, i the present tense, describing the ultimate condition, the perfect world as you see it and feel it. Remember, a perfect world is fun place to be.
    EXAMPLE: Everyone is freely expressing their own unique talent. Everyone is working in harmony. Everyone is expressing love.

4. Combine the three prior subdivisions of this paragraph into a single statement.
    EXAMPLE: My purpose is to use my creativity and enthusiasm to support and inspire others to freely express their talents in a harmonious and loving way.

Now concerning purpose elicitation; remember this quotation from the great Greek thinker Socrates;

"We are what we repeatedly do."
Benjamin Franklin's interest in books at quite an early age led him to pursue a career in the book printing and publishing industry. What is your interest? Think about what interest could be captivating your desire and how best can you turn it to a future

vocation or career. As a guide the essential condition for everything you do according to Juliette Nadia Boulanger (a French Composer) must be **choice, love and passion.**

Activity 4: **Discover your life's purpose**

1. Having seen the example, try and craft your own purpose statement. This is very important since it is your map about who you are and gives you impetus as to how to act. Building your vision around these will enable to achieve your desired goal.

5
Decide want you want - pursue your Vision/Dreams

We're all at different stages in life as to what we want to be, and have in life. Again success means different things to people. However, the process to determining what we want in life will depend on our ability to use creative imagination to perceive the future life as well being able to act on such information to make it a reality.

The formula for finding out what you really want to do is:

- To identify what is important to you
- Clarify what you want
- Decide changes to make

Look at your life as a whole - work and career, finance, recreation and free time, health and fitness, relationships, personal goals, and contribution to bigger society. Your vision will consist of a detailed description of where you want to get to. It's a detailed description of what your destination looks like and feels like. For you to creatively describe what you desire in these areas of your life you need to develop the skill of imagining your future.

The problem most of the time is that most people don't know what they want. You must be clear in your mind's eye what you want NOT what you don't want. This is the beginning of your dream, which will help to the crafting of your vision. **Some people have described dream as a goal with time and date of fulfilment. On the hand, a vision is a statement picturing a future when your goal is achieved and mission (living your purpose) accomplished**

Imagining your future – the art of visioning

Imagine yourself in five, or ten years' time from now having done something that you really want to achieve. It could be in any of those areas mentioned above. Build up your picture by imagining it to be a movie using only your sense of sight. When you've played it and noticed what you see, then play the movie again and notice what it looks like when you include sound and feelings to create a more intense image.

The Vision Exercise
"The creation of vision comes from a considerable amount of exploring, analysing, and rooting around the territory of the problem."
Mary Anne Devuma and Eliza Collins in the new portable MBA

Envision the following areas of your life –

1. Professional

2. Financial

3. Physical

4. Mental

5. Family

6. Spiritual

7. Lifestyle

Pay attention to these areas of your life and observe and think about each of them. The decisions you make will be in the present. What is happening in these areas?

- Imagine that there is a miracle tonight and you woke up in the morning and everything was the just the way you wanted it to be, how would you know it had happened?

- What would you see, hear, feel, and believe that will tel you a miracle had happened?

- What would achieving your goal give you that you do not already have?

- What action do you need to take NOW to ensure that this happens? As you can see I have deliberately inserted the word 'NOW' to emphasise the need not to procrastinate. Time is of great essence! Time is **NOW!**

- What will it take to satisfy you that you have achieved your aim and the outcome you desire? Know that whenever there unexpressed possibility or function not performed there is desire is possibility seeking expression, or function seeking performance.

- What conditions must be true for your plans to succeed?

- What sacrifices will you (or people around you) have to make?

Activity 5: **Decide want you want - pursue your Vision/Dreams**

1. Using the power of your imagination alone based on your senses envision the person you desire to become one year from now and using power of words to paint a compelling picture of this new YOU.

2. How will he/she think, feel and act?

6

The Neurological Levels of thinking

"When everything you think, do, say and believe about our capabilities to take on challenges and win aligns in the same direction as our goals, we become truly powerful."

Frances Coombes – Author Teach Yourself Self-Motivation

In this section we'll look at thinking at different levels and end their implications in our ability to achieve successful outcome towards the goals we want to complete.

Understanding thinking at these levels will enable us to continually challenge the way we look at things which in turn will impact the results we get. Therefore, we'll look at the following:

- The idea and process behind the NLP logical levels of change

- Implications of the Neurological levels of thinking to creative process

The idea and process behind the NLP logical levels of change

Thinking is a skill. It's an operational skill that enables us to develop and run with ideas, concepts, dreams and different forms of 'thought entities'. Thinking is also a skill that has to be learned as well as improved upon so as to sharpen our completion or execution acuities enabling is to deliver excellence. The idea behind the Neurological level of thinking is based on the fact that thinking is done at different levels and deliberations in these levels result to change which affect the result we get. The Neurological levels of change is a model devised by Robert Dilts based on the 'neurological levels' proposed by anthropologist Gregory Bateson.

It helps us to think through on different levels or category at a time, and capture all the additional insights gained that would otherwise have escaped. Hence from the point of view of goal setting and achieving successful outcome it helps us to articulate, visualize and execute second to non by sharpening our mental and physical attitude. When our thinking is clear then our doing becomes clearer and easy. The table below shows a table of different neurological levels of thinking on experience during a creative experience.

Identity Who?	Mission Sense of Self
Belief	Permission
Why?	Motivation
Capabilities	Strategy
How?	Plan
Behaviour	Actions
What?	Reactions
Environment	Opportunities
Where?	Constraints
When?	

Source: Adapted from; Robert B Dilts (1993) Skills for the Future – managing creativity and innovation – pp. 54-57.

In creating any experience in life there are two desires that you must align for your dream to come true. These are the mental and physical desires. The former is internal (mental) and is made up of your thoughts and ideas; and the later is physical, which consists of subsistence and propagation. For you ideals to be turned into reality these two desires must be satisfied. If you look at these levels of change, you will notice that they consist of qualities that you need in different planes of your thought process so as to accomplish a successful outcome.

A little change on your identity (who?) will have a great impact on your completion drive for a particular task or activity. It is a question of the mission in hand and an appraisal of the sense of self.

Belief asks the question of why; the permission or motivation, to move in the direction of your accomplishment.

There is the question of capability (how); the strategy and plan towards the realisation of your dream.

What ask the question of the behaviour you need tom adopt in the accomplishment of your desire. The actions and reaction necessary for the ideals that you want to achieve.

The environment is the physical plane where your actions will determine the positive outcome of your experience (where and when). This has effect in terms of time and space. You need physical and intelligent action to sustain and shape your physical environment so as to realise your dream. There are also issues of opportunities and constraints.

In the next chapter, think about the effect of these neurological levels of thinking on mindset and their impact towards any accomplishment.

Activity 6: **The Neurological Levels of thinking**

1. Critically appraise the Neurological levels of thinking and tease out the impact

   it had on a past project.

2. Did you accomplish it? If not evaluate why based on your recent

   understanding of these levels of change,

3. Armed with this new understanding what adjustments do you need to make

   towards a present task or project?

7
The Success Mindset – Be-Do- Have formulae for success
"Being mastery –oriented is about having the right-mindset."
Carol S Dweck – PhD Professor of Psychology at Stanford

Did you know that the most successful people in any work of life have shaped their mind in a particular way that seeks supports and help them get what they want?

Success is a practice. It's an experience that results in whom you have become as a result

of what you do and have. Success has it rewards. In this section we're going to look at how

three dynamics – your being, what you do, and what you have impact on success.

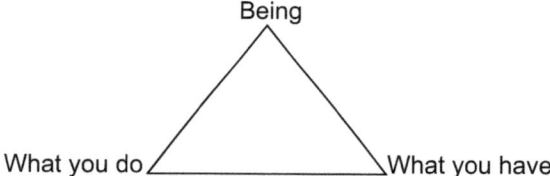

The above are the three processes for developing a success mind set. These parts could be

cultivated in different stages in your quest for success journey or creative endeavour. But

suffice it that success is who you've become. I've to demonstrate this framework by telling

this motivating story.

The Young Girl's Dream

It was the story of a young girl who had a dream; to be accepted in the Melbourne

Conservatory as a professional musician. This vision was heart felt and consuming.

Her friends were whiling away their time in trivial pursuit; like watching DVD's and eating

pizza the young girl practiced her music. She practiced for about 4 -5 hours every day. In

2008, she was accepted into the Conservatory.

In this story, it will be seen that her vision provided her with the specifics – the what, the

when and how of accomplishment.

The New Habit

Connecting her conscious and her subconscious (formed her habits; **a way of being.** It's internal and does impact all you're able to do or achieve. And the ability to say no to the DVD and pizza!

These changed what she did and hence the outcome – becoming a professional musician and membership to the prestigious Melbourne Conservatory.

This short story in a nutshell shares how to develop the success mind-set. It is the ability to modify your behaviour and adopt those that can help you to model success.

Modelling other people's skill

When successful people are involved in activities that they are used to, they have some attributes as well as drivers or cues that propel them to successful outcome. Understanding these qualities and being able to model them is important to developing the particular mind set.

What are the behaviours that they exhibit?

What is their belief behind these behaviours?

What's their state of mind?

What type of sensory awareness did they adopt?

You'll also be able to master the drivers of successful people behaviour:

- Skills
- Tools and techniques they used
- Personal beliefs and what they were doing.
- Plan and strategies that they embrace

Activity 7: **The Success Mindset – Be-Do- Have formulae for success**

1. What is the venture or process that you desire to be successful in recently or in the future?

2. Appraise who you need to be so as to achieve your outcome?

3. How can you cultivate a growing mind-set as opposed to a fixed one?

8
Six Habits that leads to success
Success leaves clues
Anthony Robbins –Author of Unlimited Power

In our waking hours we perform three different types of activities - our thoughts, feelings and our actions or behaviours which impact the results that we get from life. Habits are the results of the cumulative effects of these normal life processes. Some habits are good and others are not so good. The outcome is that the good habits enable us to achieve our potential and the bad one are limiting; in that they hinder our progress in diverse ways.

In this section we'll look at the role Neuro Linguistic Programming (NLP) has to play in optimising our potential through modelling and adopting the behaviour of high performers in different works of life.

The following are the snap short behaviours that will enable us to achieve success if we learn and apply them in our success journey. It was created from neuro linguistic programming (NLP) – which studies the human achievements and behaviours that goes with attainment.

1. Start with the end in mind. It was Stephen Covey that suggested that you begin with the end in mind. In creating the success that you deserve, you need to decide exactly the result or outcome that you desire. What would you see to know that you have attained the outcome? How will you manage the processes required to the realization of the outcome you want? What are the tasks, activities, resources (time, money, skill set, knowledge and human), and how they fit into the overall scheme.

2. Use your eyes and senses. We take in information from the world by making use of our senses – see, hear, taste and touch. This is the basis of the sense

perception process. Perception is projection; meaning that our experience is a direct representation of our consciousness. The effect of the patterning of information resulting from our sensory acuity when sharpened could help us see experience in new light.

3. If what you doing are not working – try something else. We always receive feedback as a result of our actions or behaviours. If what we are doing is not producing the result or outcome we want we need to review, evaluate, and determine the reason for the result we are getting. We then have to take action and change our behaviour or the habit that has led us to the outcome. Therefore, we need to be flexible and prepare to change the behaviour to whatever is necessary to reach a desired or successful outcome. Being flexible has to do with being able to be more fluent to using different thinking styles that suits the situation at hand.

4. Build and maintain rapport with yourself and others. We need to improve in the way we communicate with ourselves and therefore with other people. Building rapport will stem from the realization of the how we relate and communicate with others and this knowledge will impact the way we communicate with others. Creating a relationship of trust and co-operation is paramount here. This ability will put us in a better position to communicate, collaborate and cooperate with others in the bid to drive initiatives forward.

5. Operate from a state of excellence. Operating in a position of excellence will result from putting in place the other requirement needed for success – sensory awareness, planning your outcome, building rapport, and being prepared to change your behaviour to get what you want. This is the basis of operating from a totally resourceful state. Develop the habit of chunking –

breaking your objectives into small manageable steps and build to bigger goals gradually. This has a way of boosting your confidence as it will empower you to make progress to your desired outcome.

6. Take action. Having done all, nothing happen without action. Remember an idea is a notion, unless an action is taken. We need to have the determination and commitment to move forward with our ideas to make our dreams a reality.

Six habits the lead to success

How to deal with failure
"Failure is, in a sense the highway to success, inasmuch as every discovery of what is false leads us to seek earnestly what is true."
-John Keats

Success is a habit so also is failure. We feel terrible at the sound of the word 'failure.' Failure is an experience; for us to make good use of the experience we nee to learn from the experience. If we are courageous and confident in our success journey we need to welcome failure and learn the lesson from it. Successful people fail forward. What does it mean? They work on the premise that there is no failure but feedback. They take failure as a feedback to a process that has been flawed. In other to make progress they analyse the situation and use the feedback as basis for further experience.

Below is a summary of different themes that can be applies in any experience of failure so as to benefit from the experience.

- See failure as an experience

- Analyze the experience

- Find the lesson they taught

- It's possible that the time invested to study failure could lead to success. This possible by applying the feedback as information for further practice

- Mastering the art of dealing with failure could become the basis of converting defeat as a stepping stone for opportunity

The diagram below taken from the book "Teach yourself leadership" by Catherin Doherthy and John Thompson describes how to deal with failure.

There is no failure

Only

Receive feedback   ——————▶   FEEDBACK —————— 'Thank you'

↓

DATA

↓

AWARENESS

↓

CHOICE ———— **Consequence**

Give feedback

◀————— DEVELOP & GROW

The feedback loop

The diagram suggests that there is no failure but feedback. The outcome or result should be treated as data so as to become aware or the reason for the outcome. On proper evaluation of the circumstance, you have to decide on the choice to make. Either to follow through and gain experience that will enable you to perform better next time – develop and grow, or just do nothing. The result is for having a feedback is then fed into the loop. The application of the result will helps you to perform better next time.

How Dale Carnegie used failure as learning experience to become a success

If you think that most of the successful men you hear about today had always found the success landscape easy; then you have to think again. To be successful you need to develop the ability to learn from your mistakes. There are very important principles which most successful people have understood and this makes it possible for them to succeed where others seem to have failed. In his book Awaken the Giant Within; he called it "The Ultimate Success Formula", and is made of the following steps:

1. Decide what you want
2. Take action
3. Notice what's working or not, and
4. Change your approach until you achieve what you want

The inspirational story of how Carnegie followed this idea to succeed was told by John C Maxwell in his book "Your Road Map for Success." It was a story fold by Giles Kemp and Edward Claflin in their book: Dale Carnegie – The Man Who Influenced Millions.

How did someone whose early life was plagued with failure become worldwide phenomena with success?

He grew up in poverty. He was so poor that when he decided to go teachers college in Warrensburg, Missouri, he lived at home and was riding to school each day on horseback.

He was interested in public speaking from his teens, so Carnegies decided that he wanted t earn recognition at the college by entering speech contests. He never won a single competition, but learned each time he tried and failed.

Despite his hard work at the college, he failed to graduate when he didn't pass Latin. He then moved from Maryville Missouri, to New York City, where he tried acting and sales, but success was still cut short.

Dale then got up cut up with a golden opportunity. He applied for a job at the YCMA to teach classes in public speaking. Because he lacked the experience, the YCMA didn't offer him the usual salary of two dollar per session. He was accepted on a trial basis. The condition for his continued employment was that: if he was effective and retained students, he would earn money. If not, he would loss his job.

Though he ha failed to win a speech contest or become successful as an actor, he succeeded at the YCMA. He realised his teenage dream of becoming a public speaker. Those early detours according to John Maxwell had taught him a lot. Soon he was developing his own courses and writing pamphlets the he would later publish as books. In their book Kemp and Claflin had to say this about him:"Carnegie rose to fame as one of the most effective trainers of speakers and one of the best-selling authors of all time. Two keys enabled him to turn failure into success: his **unwillingness to be stopped by failure, and his unwillingness to learn from failure.**

Moreover he secretly followed the ultimate success formula: **decided what he wanted, took action, and noticed what's working or not, and, changed his approach until he achieves what he wanted.**

Today the name Carnegie is synonymous with success. His Dale Carnegie Institute for Effective Speaking and Human Relations currently trains people all over the world. His book How to Win Friends and Influence People has sold for more than fifteen million copies and continues to sell sixty years after it was established.

In a nutshell successful people have **great attitude** to hang on in their success journey, enjoying the experience on the way knowing that the process is as important as the end, if not better.

Activity 8: **Six Habits that leads to success**

1. Study a person or individual within the circle of your profession who has achieved great success. Keep a note of the attributes responsible for their great accomplishment.

2. Read a biography of a successful person you admire. What do you think has prepared them for the great life that they live?

Part 3: Success Actions

"There is only one thing that makes a dream impossible to achieve: the fear of failure." - David Deida

Success could be said to take place in two planes – the mental and the physical. The mental aspect of making your dream come true requires that you are able to take control of your environment. In this respect you are talking about where and when. The environment where you execute your dream is of great essence so also is the timing. For you to execute second to none; you should be aware of the behaviour you need to adopt so as to pull off a competent and excellent performance. It is important to point out here that how you have performed in the mental side is importance to how well you perform.

Different tools – clear articulation of your objectives through setting SMART goals, planning, time management and possession of positive emotional attitudes were also explored.

9

The Power of Goal Setting

"If you want to be happy set a goal that commands your thoughts, liberates your energy, and inspires your hopes."
Andrew Carnegie – The richest man in America in the early 1900s

According to Nick James – Internet Information Marketer; "A goal is nothing more than a name given to something we want to get benefit from."

Goal setting gives you insight, direction and impetus to what you want to get done or achieve. Goal setting is a skill that when mastered will help you to achieve more and become successful in your completion drive. As thinking and doing tool it enables you to develop as a thinker and doer. It helps you to use both parts of the brain because it allows developing strategies, process, tactics and focus to your dreams, intentions and ideas.

It is important to mention that for goal setting to be effective it has to be written. This is because a goal properly set is halfway reached and a goal written is set. In his book, "Your road map to success". John C Maxwell, Pastor and Leadership expert, suggested that , the process of writing down goals helps you to clarify what you intend to do, understand then importance of of your goals, and ci=omit yourself to making it happen. Hence, writing your goals maes you more accountable.

In this section we'll look as the following:

SMART Goal Setting

Additional Ingredients to make SMART Goals Work

SMART Goal Setting

SMART is an acronym for goal setting strategy which describes the step you need to achieve the result you desire. It helps you to work through clear goals and outcomes since they are written outlines for plan of action.

In setting SMART goal you start with the ain in mind. An aim is an objective, a marker, an outcome on the way to final achievement. Each outcome is made consists of sub-outcomes which helps on the journey to the final achievement. An end is the final outcome or goal.

According to the SMART model your goal should be:

Specific	A short, specific, simple description of the outcome you want.
Measurable	Goals should be measurable, meaningful to you. There should be more than one way to achieve it.
Achievable	Describe the goals in the present tense, as if they are happening now and are achieve able.
Realistic	Your goals should be responsible, realistic and right for you
Timeframe	State a time frame in which you will achieve your goals.

Source: Coombes, F (2008), Teach Yourself: Self Motivation, Hodder Education London

To be excellent i anything you do, you your goal must be to become conscious of your thinking processes and actions you take that spring from them. Always evaluate your results and seek opportunities for improvement.

Additional Ingredient to make SMART Goals Work

Having set the your goal using the SMART Method, you need to look into these three important ingredients that will help you to chat your goal to completion;

- Means
- Motives
- Opportunity

Means

Make sure you have the required skill, time, money and special knowledge that will help you to achieve your goal.

Motives

How motivated are you to see your goal to the end? Staring is one thing that commitment and determination to hang to your dream despite the difficulties along te way is very important. You should be prepared not to waiver or distracted from your goal and to follow through until completion.

Opportunity

In looking at the opportunity facing you, think in terms of the benefit that will result from taking this action and this will have the magic of sustaining your curiosity to hanging on. You need to have the power to influence the outcome of you goal and also the flexibility to tailor the outcome to suit the demands in the case of changing situations in the operational process.

Obstacles stopping you to realise your goals

Setting goals to reaching our desired outcome is one thing, actually realising the purpose that you set out to achieve is another. It's important to be aware of these hindrances that could stop us in achieving our goal. According to Jack

Canfield in his book: "How to Get from Where You Are to where you want to be-

The 25 Principles of Success."; these are:

- Considerations
- Fears
- Roadblocks

Considerations – these are due to out own thoughts about the task at hand. Most of the time, they are the results of negative thoughts which may be due to lack of confidence or courage to proceed with the goal. Knowing these forms of thinking is important because the best way to solve this problem is to transform these thoughts is to make them more empowering.

For example, let's say that you've set a goal to run a marathon and have planned you activities and tasks toward achieving it. And on the morning that you are about to start your training, you have these thoughts going through mind:

"How are you sure that you won't faint if you go out to run this morning?"

First you have to understand that these questions are subconsciously stopping you from achieving your goal. You have to challenge the question by making it more empowering. Say for example, that you'll not faint but with each distance you run will develop more inner strength which will impact on your stamina.

Fear

This barrier or obstacle operates in the realm of your feelings. Fear is nothing but feeling. Fear could come from these areas: fear of failure, fear of hurting your self both physically and emotionally, fear of rejection and fear of making a fool of your self. On the whole fear makes you want to remain in your comfort zone preventing you from experiencing expansion and growth.

In her book, "Feel the fear and do it anyway – How to turn you fear and indecision into confidence and action."'; Dr Susan Jeffers stated that fear is an experience every goal achiever faces, but those who go on to achieve their dreams have realised how to handle fear. You need to position yourself in a position of power instead of pain. According to her, we're always faced with in our decision making moments. It's our choice to put ourselves in a position of power rather than pain.

How we hold fear determines the experience we have in a given situation or event where a response is required. This is summarised in the table below:

HOW WE HOLD FEAR	
Pain	Power
Helplessness--Choice	
Depression-- Excitement	
Paralysis --Action	

Source: Adapted from **Jeffers. S** (2011); Arrow Books London, p.34

From the table above being able to hold fear in any situations is to put ourselves in a position of power. This has to do with our deal with our thought, feelings and action. We need to move ourselves consciously towards the right and the degree to which we are able to do this determines the pain or power we feel in any given experience. It's a learning process and being aware of it and consistently desiring to use this knowledge will determine how successful and happy we become.

Learn from other people's experience of dealing with fear for example the Psalmist:

"Whenever I am afraid; I will trust in You" (Psalm 56:3).

"Knowing what must be done does away with fear."
- **Rosa Parks**

Roadblocks

These are obstacles outside of us. They are not involved with our cognitive process. It could range from new developments outside of your environment to lack of support from people who you thought would have helped you in the execution your project. It's important that you know these changes can occur and that experiencing then is just a wake up call to take alternative action towards the realisation of your goal.

Activity 9: The Power of Goal Setting

1. Write you thought on the habit of goal settings?

2. Is it a habit that you have cultivated? If not; why?

3. What allowance do you need to make so as to begin to set and write down your goals?

10

Success Is Action
"Think like a man of action, and act like a man of thought."
- Henri Bergson

All the tools and techniques – crafting of purpose, taking responsibility, dream/vision, goal setting, and the neurological levels of thinking will amount to nothing without effective, focused and strategic actions to make the dream a reality. Taking action towards your journey to the desired outcome will require moving out of your comfort zone to the unknown destination.

Wallace D Wattle reasoned that: by thought the things you want is brought to you, by action you receive them. This statement is in line with the scripture that faith without work is dead!

It's a risk taking, requires effort (mental and physical), focus and discipline, courage, commitment and determination, resources (money, skill sets, time (yours and other people's), and varying forms of resistance – considerations, fears (failure, success, change, being different etc.) and roadblocks. These experiences if uncontrolled could greatly have impact on the outcome we want.

Goal achievement is not wishful thinking; you have to be persuaded that you have the ability to achieve these goals. Remembering that the goal has to be very definitive in terms of what need to be achieved and by how much (metrics) and when (date and time).

On the whole you have to have great positive mental attitude that you are able to successfully achieve your goal by applying yourself. This requires discipline, commitment and determination. Taking action involves the manipulation of our physical environment so as to achieve the result we desire.

I love the take that Wallace D Wattles had on his book "How to get what you want." He is of the opinion that success is getting what you want and is an effect, occurring from the application of a cause. For you to succeed you need to be fully persuaded that you are to succeed. It is important that you have your mind attuned to the regime and requirements for success. Here your subconscious and objective mind must be in agreement: know what to do and how to do it. **He called this a state of power and poise, faith, conscious power in action or simply active power consciousness.** You also need to start from where you are using what you have in your present environment as you move forward to achieve your future desire.

Success in anything is not about talk, it's about action
Benjamin Franklin

Some techniques to enhance the execution of your goals:

The power of decision

A story was told of a retiring successful bank president, whom a reporter asked the secrets to his success. He replied:

"That's easy to answer: good decisions."

"And what do you attribute your good decisions?"

"That's easier still: the wisdom gained from experience."

"And where did you get that experience?"

"Easy again; bad decisions!"

Decision taking is a cause and effect relationship. The idea here is that for every decision we take we set loose a cause in motion which comes with it an effect in the direction of our goal or destiny. Decision taking is very important because it is the gateway to the creation of our desired outcome. Moreover the action we take or not in any situation, results in an outcome. Different actions produce different results and these are due to the power of decisions. When we take action we physically manipulate the environment. When we think, we mentally manipulate internal representations of objects, activities and situations. Thinking is possible because our internal representations simplify and summarise information.

Anthony Robbins in his book: "Awaken the giant within" has this to say about:

"Making a true decision means, committing to achieving a result, and then cutting yourself off from any other possibility."

He was of the opinion that, information is power when acted upon, and one of his criteria for a true decision is that ACTION flows from it.

For our decisions to be effective, it has to focus on three mains areas:

1. Your decision about what you focus on – perception
2. Your decision about what things mean to you – process
3. Your decision about what to do to create the result you desire – performance

How successful you become in life depends on how you develop mastery in taking effective decisions along these areas mentioned above. Remember, that decision taking is a skill and like most skills, you will become fluent with practice.

Some barriers in decision making and how to deal with them

Most of us find it very easy to make decision, whereas others find it very difficult. Some of the things that may get in the way of the process:

- fear and anxieties;

- availability of information and other resources;

- conflicting time scales;

- the behaviour of others

Fear and anxieties

Fear has be mentioned else where as on of the feelings that does affect our moving on with our goals. The key thing is to be aware that everyone faces fear, but how we manage it is very important. We feel the fear but, take the decision anyway! On clear symptom of fear is procrastination. Some of the reasons for procrastination include:

- fear of failing or making a mistake;

- boredom;

- uncertainty over how to go about a task;

- anxiety about possible consequence of your action;

- perfectionism – unwillingness to start a task unless it can be completed perfectly.

The antidote is to follow the path to power - see page 60, how we hold fear.

Information

Information at any level of decision taking process is very important. Having the right information is one thing and being able to analyse it so as to extract the relevant data to help us make the right decision is also very important. The key point here is to weigh the outcome of the decision in terms of benefits – usually in long term.

Timing

The aspect of timing and window of opportunity is very important. Every decision we take has a time element to it. Time is an indispensable and scarce resource that needs to be managed effectively. There is also need to take care about having all the evidence within the limited time so as not to rush into wrong decisions. In looking at time, it will be important to look at the short, medium and long term implications of the decisions we take.

The behaviour of others

Sometimes the decisions that we take could impact other in different ways. Therefore, there is the need to involve all those who will be involved in the decision making process and share the idea of such decisions with them. The key point in this circumstance is to share the benefit of the decision with those involved so as to enable them buy into the project – take ownership.

Establish a plan and track your time

What is a plan? A plan is a method of action, procedure or arrangement. It is a program to be done. It is a design to give effect to an idea, a thought, a project or development of something. A plan asks questions concerning things – ideas, process or people. For example: it may ask what do you desire? Do you desire to sell something? Do you desire to build a house? Do you desire a job? Do you desire an increase in salary? Do you desire clients? Do you desire customers? Do you to invent something? **These questions pertain to your present and future occupation**.

According to Wallace D Wattle; "Whenever there is unexpressed possibility or function not performed, there is unsatisfied desire. **Desire is possibility seeking expression, or function seeking performance."**

Earl Prevette reasoned that the only way to make your desire known is through a plan. It conveys to people in plain language a definite concept of what you are offering for their consideration. Clarity is power. If you fail to plan you plan to fail.

Peter Drucker Management expert explained that planning defines the particular place you want to be and how you intend to get there. Planning does not substitute facts for judgement nor science of leadership it recognises the importance of analysis, courage, experience, intuition – even hunch. It is responsibility rather than technique. Planning is not an event. It is the continuous process of strengthening what works and abandoning what does not, of taking risk – taking decisions with the greatest knowledge of their potential effect, of setting objectives, appraising performance and results through systematic feedback, and making on going adjustment as conditions change.

Having set forth the plan to accomplish your objectives which is made of loads of tasks and different activities which requires different time slots for their accomplishments; you need to apportion time to the tasks proportionately. There is time for everything under the sum. Time uses us, so to be effective in our use of time as to achieve more, we need to have a planning system to keep track of time and activities. Perhaps this advice from Benjamin Franklin who is called the Father of Time Management because of his great accomplishments would suffix:

"We must recognise the most precious thing any person has is his or her time. Time is money. Time is the stuff of which life is made. And time must be cherished, for productive purposes and always with frugality."

One of the most fundamental lessons on time is that:

Time is now; therefore time is the present. There is never any time but now. If you want to begin to make ready for their reception of what you want begin now.

Have the right frame of mind – mental attitude

Having the right mental attitude involves a series of positive emotional feelings, moods or attitude that will enable you to marry the world of imagination and reality. The right mental attitude could be described as the 'can do' attitude. It means that if you believe that you can do it, you can whereas if you don't believe in the achievement of your goal you won't. It's like self-fulfilling prophesy. Some of the desired mental attitude is determination and commitment to the realisation of one's goal. This poem aptly captures the idea of having a positive mental attitude. It was taken from "Think and Grow Rich", by Napoleon Hill:

If you think you are beaten, you are

If you think you dare not, you don't

If you like to win, but you think you can't

It is almost certain you won't

If you think you'll lose, you're lost

For out of the world we find that, success begins with a fellow's will-

It's all in the state of mind

If you think you are outclassed, you are

You've got to think high to rise

You've got TO be sure of yourself before

You can ever win a prize

"Life's battle don't always to to the stronger or faster man

But sooner or later the man who wins

Is the man WHO THINKS HE CAN"

You need to have an attitude of faith and purpose.

Develop flexible thinking skills

On the difference between little tasks and big tasks: Warren Hilton author of Positive Psychology said; **"Big things are little things put together."**

Flexible thinking is the ability to apply integrative thinking whereby you become fluent in the ability to the creative (imaginative) side – right hemisphere and the logical (detail) side – left hemisphere of the brain. It leads to empowerment of your cognitive and emotional stakes. As a big picture thinker you can see the whole picture with your imaginative eye as well as breaking them into smaller parts. The technique is known as chunking.

This idea is illustrates below:

Big picture thinker

Chunking down – detail thinker

Effective time management skills –

Since you work in a given time and space, it's very important to understand how you deal with time. This will help you to leverage your outcome – the speed and outcome of you effort. Some of the time management principles are basically based on our ability to prioritise and deliver second to none in terms of output. It is a management technique which focuses on how we can intelligently use our time to achieve more. Principally, we need to be able to break the tasks requires to complete a particular project in to activities with time constraints (duration). This is at the heart of project management. These activities could be broken into urgent, important, to do list and note.

The urgent – refers to immediate tasks that must be done to make things happen in the future.

Important – things that you are setting up to happen next

To do – the standard things you must do around tasks and events to make things happen, say for example, book a room for an event, thank a speaker, buy consumables towards an evening meal.

Note – things that are coming up in the future that you need to be aware of, and may be gather information and prepare for.

To completely leverage your time when completing a task, remember that 80% 0f the returns of your daily 'to do' list will come from 20% of the items you have listed and often from just one item. This is the basis of the Pareto principle.

- Focus on the most important task, even though it may be urgent

- Ask yourself: "Which of these tasks relate directly to my goals?"

"Which of these still matters in 5 years from now?"

Pareto principle (80/20)

In 1906, Italian economist Vilfredo Pareto created a mathematical formula to describe the unequal distribution of wealth in his country, observing that twenty percent of the people owned eighty percent of the wealth. In the late 1940s, Dr. Joseph M. Juran inaccurately attributed the 80/20 Rule to Pareto, calling it Pareto's Principle. While it may be misnamed, Pareto's Principle or Pareto's Law as it is sometimes called can be a very effective tool to help you manage effectively.

After Pareto made his observation and created his formula, many others observed similar phenomena in their own areas of expertise. Quality Management pioneer, Dr Joseph Juran, working in the US in the 1930s and 40s recognized a universal principle he called the "vital few and trivial many" and reduced it to writing. In an early work, a lack of precision on Juran's part made it appear that he was applying Pareto's observations about economics to a broader body of work. The name Pareto's Principle stuck, probably because it sounded better than Juran's Principle. As a result, Dr. Juran's observation of the "vital few and trivial many", the principle that 20 percent of something always are responsible for 80 percent of the results, became known as Pareto's Principle or the 80/20 Rule.

Pareto's Principle, the 80/20 Rule, should serve as a daily reminder to focus 80 percent of your time and energy on the 20 percent of your work that is really important. **Don't just "work smart", work smart on the right things.**

Review your progress

You need to develop strategies to monitor the progress of your goals. You may need to keep a goal book where you log the activities and the action plan as well as who is responsible to carry out the task and by what time.

Develop the habit of reading and rereading your goal three times a day. The idea for repetitions is to condition your subconscious mind and unleash the creative powers to help you make you goals a reality. Jack Canfield suggested that you make it a habit to review your goals at least twice a day – in the morning upon waking up and in the night before going to bed. You can also write them down on a 3" x 5" index card, which you can take along with you wherever you go so as to be able to review your goal morning and night.

You can put a list of your goals on a daily planner or a calendar system. With the availability of different information storing systems in the computer, you can create a pop-up screen saver in your computer of the list of your goals. The whole idea is that of visibility and to keep your goal in mind in front of you continuously.

Being prompt to change any thing that is necessary will help to speed time to accomplish your goal.

Activity 10: **Success Is Action**

1. What actions do you need to take today for the success that you desire tomorrow?

2. What are the reasons stopping you?

3. How can you effectively handle the treat these experiences create to your realizing your dream?

Part 4: Success Exemplars
"Success is a matter of sticking to a set of principles anyone can master" – Earl Nightingale, Author, Lead the Field

In this section we are going to look at some of the tested and proven habits use by successful people to duplicate or leverage their success geometrically. Developing these habits and applying them in you individual life or business will place you in another level: above your peers. The key theme here is that you need to invest in yourself anyway you deem possible so as to create a state of growth and abundance.

Some of the tools used by experts in the field of personal develop are highlighted, and how they can impact your output in terms of productivity evaluated.

As usual there are activities to do at the end of each chapter.

11

Create your own blue print for success – a practical guide

"If you go to work with your goals, your goals will go to work with you. If you go to work with your plan, your plan will go to work with you. Whatever good things we build end up building us."

Jim Rohn – American Foremost Business Philosopher

Success is a journey and takes place at three levels:

- The things you choose to focus on in life

- The meaning or interpretation you put upon the information you receive

- The action you take as a result of processing that information

For us to be in control of the results or outcome we have in life, we need to be in control of these three departments mentioned above. What it entails is that we develop mastery in the way we think. Thinking is a skill that can be mastered if we put effort to understanding it as a discipline. For us to be truly successful there is need for the concentration of the power of thought and directing the thought through planned action towards a particular goal.

In a nutshell judging from the above descriptions of levels of success, we have to look at success based on the following sub themes:

- The things you choose to focus in life – perception

- The meaning or interpretation you put upon the information – processing

- The action you take as a result of processing the information – performance

The things you choose to focus in life - perception

- What do you focus on in life? The way you perceive things is based on how you use your senses to focus on things. Ii is made up up what you focus on as well as how you focus. The important thing here is the role your senses play in focusing on what is important to you in your immediate environment as this will impact on the things your neurological system will be geared to work on. If you liken this aspect of the transaction between the environment and the brain in a given system as the input; it does impact what is processed. Therefore your level of awareness as to what you want observes and how you want to observe it comes into play here.

The meaning or interpretation you put upon the information – processing (organisation)

Meaning making or interpretation of information is an internal construct. It takes place in the brain within the association neurons. Essentially, the aspect of information processing depends a lot on reference that has already being stored in the brain and with the help of the information already available in the brain the brain tries to make sense of the information through association. This stage is very important in our decision making process because the information will be sent to the action neurons so as to elicit particular action. It is important the decision making process is make at the conscious level where the individual has the ability to make use of myriad of information in the present circumstance for making decision not based on the old habit (the unconscious mind).

The action you take as a result of processing the information – performance

This is the last stage where the thinking process finishes and the output of the information is played out in the environment by the elicitation of the action neurones sending signals to then glands and muscles for specific action. This point is very critical because you can decide to either take action or not take action. Either way the result will be played out in long term. It is important to realise to that we need to take physical action so as to manipulate our physical environment. This culminates the fact that thinking is both mental and physical effort.

Steps to reach your goals

Being successful begin by becoming aware and responsible for our thinking and action resulting from it. We need to have faith that it is us that will make our dream come true – trusting God. Hence this section will summarise the step we can take to accomplish anything we desire to do, The principle here is service follow, success and rewards (money, fame, achievement): <service – success – rewards>

The following steps below have been suggested by Vic Johnson – goal setting expert:

1. Have a clear picture of your burning desire – You need to have a very clear vision of what it is that you want; not what you don't want. This is the beginning of your dream. Here your imagination is meant to be brought into action.

2. Write a statement of definite purpose – you have to be able to write down this desire succinctly in writing as a very clear objective. For example if you nee to purchase a car you need to write it down so that the purpose is clear to be actionable. An example could be that I need to purchase or buy a black Mercedes car – C220 model. If on the other hand you want some money; you need to be able to state the exact amount. It could even be you desire to have a particular grade in your examination. No matter what, the idea is the same.

3. Decide what you will give in return for your success – What do you need to give in return for your success. This principle of contribution. Remember that that rewards - follow service, getting follow - giving, and making an impression - follow making a difference. There is no such thing as getting something for nothing. Just at the time of this writing I received a cheque from the post for a sum of money from the HM Revenue and Customs. It was due to repayment of income tax for tax year 2010 – 2011. This benefit will not have been possible without my contribution in excess of what is required from me. This idea here is to set into motion an action that will result in the experience that you want. Remember that there is no such thing as something for nothing. Service follows success and success money (or any scorecard to measure success). What are you prepared to give in return for what you desire?

4. Set a date for the accomplishment of your goal – You need to clearly set a date for the accomplishment of your goal. What you need to achieve, when and by how much? Remember that a dream is a goal without a completion date. Having a date propels you to have the conviction and self-confidence to make your dream a reality.

5. Write down your plan where it can be added and modified as needed – You need to explicitly write down your plan of action. You have to note that it is not written in stone and that you have to be flexible enough to create changes as they arise.

6. Write an affirmation statement that tricks the subconscious into thinking you have already attained your burning desire – An affirmation is a statement that describes a goal in its already completed state. For example: "I am enjoying driving my new black Mercedes C220 saloon." It's like counting your chicks

before they are hatched. It should be in the present tense and positively stated. Read the statement s at least twice a day, morning and night – Reading the statement day and night is a reminder to your inner man of the new experience that you are living in. It's a way of conditioning and creates an opportunity for meditation. Continuously you are reminding your inner man of the new experience that you desire to create.

7. Change your environment and surround yourself with symbols that remind you of your goal and resemble your life once you achieve it – You have to remember that thinking is in two levels – physical and mental: and both require effort. The manipulation of your physical environment is the action that you'll take to create the physical environment to the desired state that you've envisaged. This processional effect is one way to manipulate your environment to the desired final state.

David Lewis has this take on the thinking in action; that without the ability to act effectively the most creative thought, inspired idea, brilliant concept, and startling theory of great vision will have no meaning. That the individual has to assume responsibility for its successful and vigorous implementation, or it will never see the light of day. Therefore there is the need to marry the world of imagination and the world of reality. This is made possible through sticking a balance between the two worlds in terms of resources – the former is filled with endless possibilities and boundless resources and the later has finite resources and still with less of that most important commodity - 'time.'

In his book, *how to turn ability to cash*; Earl Prevette, gave very insightful view and advice on how to turn an idea to reality. This is summarised here:

1. Understand the principle of the knowledge for the plan.

2. Establish the law to process the plan and turn it into action. These laws are:

- Law of faith – to believe the plan wholeheartedly

- Law of Repetition – to perfect it

- Law of Imagination – to visualise it

- Law of Persistence – to see it through

- Law of Action – to idealise the plan to feel its possession and claim it as reality.

3. The Act of making the Plan a reality – this requires sustained and focused effort, energy and channelling all the resources' you have within your power towards making your dream a reality.

Activity 11: **Create your own blue print for success – a practical guide**

1. Success in life is becoming what you want to be. What is that you want to achieve/become?

2. With the blue print for successes you have read develop a compelling evident to act a guide to creating what you want to achieve. Just base it on one idea.

12

Three Success Principles you need to master so as succeed in Life

There is no such thing as secret as some people will want you to believe. However, for you to make success a habit there is something that you know that others don't which makes it possible for you to put up excellent performances. The key idea here is that for you to develop success consciousness there are three things mentioned by Anthony Robbins in his book; "Awaken the Giant Within" that you need to learn to do:

1. Raise your standard
2. Change your limiting beliefs
3. Change your strategy

Raise your standards

What does it mean to raise your standard? Simply, it refers to the things you will no longer accommodate in your life. It is sought of changing your mind. Change is not easy. But suffix it that change is possible if you make up your mind to change. Change is also profitable, because it is a nature process that transforms the state of things for good or bad. But as it concerns us human beings, the most important change is in the way we think. Thinking is a discipline that can be learned. Changing the way we think about things is an investment in you. We can intentionally purpose to raise our standard of life by changing the way we think. Raising your standards and therefore changing yourself will not only profit you but also those around you. This is because in order to raise your standard - increase your potential: you need to change your thinking. This could be as simple as changing the way you think about a particular thing, person or piece of information. This will in turn impact your general feelings about the situation or event with the result that your attitude and hence your experience is positively enhanced.

Change your limiting beliefs

The key thing about raising your standards is to change your thinking. Changed thinking results in changed belief. What is belief? Belief is faith or certainty or conviction that what you desire to achieve will eventually happen.

 In the scripture Hebrews 11:1:

"Faith is the substance of things hoped for and the evidence of things not seen."

What are the limiting beliefs that have negative impact for you to achieve your dream? You need to be able to identify them and get rid of them. Part of identifying them is to become self-aware and responsible for the accomplishment of your dream. These limiting beliefs impact on your self-confidence to achieve your goal. There are considerations, fear and obstacles that stop you from moving forward (see pages 31-33). They can operate at mental or physical levels. At the mental level you need to appraise the way you think and on the environmental level you may develop mastery on techniques, skills and strategies to manipulate your physical environment.

Even though these limiting belief are within or without, the first thing is to know that they are there. The next thing is to shift or move away from the pattern of behaviour resulting from them and to develop the patterns of behaviours that empower us and drive us towards our goals. You need to develop as many references as possible as to why your present belief is empowering and develop further references from within and around you until the desires situation is believable. As a Christian you can faithfully speak forth the word of faith concerning the situation. For example:

"I can do all things through Christ who strengthens me."

These limiting beliefs could come in from of insight or renewed knowledge or mind set. It gives you the impetus to see the situation in new light and the power to act decisively. Any thing that makes that which is hidden to be manifest is light. Seek insight in your thinking, feeling and action you had responded to the situation in the past. Now realise that the past is gone and that the action you take in the present moment to adopt a new belief system through changed thinking will great y impact your future circumstance.

Choose empowering beliefs to disempowering beliefs.

Change your strategy
"Tactics are the servant of strategy the overall goal and guideline are set by strategy."
-    **Edward de Bono – Thinker and Writer**

What is strategy? **Strategy**, a word of military origin, refers to a plan of action designed to achieve a particular goal. In military usage strategy is distinct from tactics, which are concerned with the conduct of an engagement, while strategy is concerned with how different engagements are linked (http://en.wikipedia.org/wiki/Strategy).

Changing your strategy will come from changing you thinking in areas where it is not working. Develop new thinking habits that are profitable and learn to imitate the thinking habits of great achievers. Your success or failure in any endeavour depends on your strategy. Those who succeed follow a strategy so also are those who fail. Therefore you need to study and apply the strategies used by peak performers in the skill that you need to master. This is known as modelling. It is easier today to follow particular individuals so as to understand the way they accomplish great things. In his book " Awaken the giant within"; Anthony Robbins described them as 'organising principles'. These organising principles will enable you to keep your commitment in the bid to making your dream come true. It means that you need to commit yourself to lifelong learning; after all how can you change your strategy if you have none in your repertoire of strategies.

Activity 12: **Three Success Principles you need to master so as succeed in Life**

1. What is it that you desired to achieve recently?

2. Did you achieve it?

3. If No; why didn't you and if yes how?

4. Critically evaluate your methods and try to find out the reasons why you succeeded where you deed.

5. List some of the attributes you think are required for us to make success of any endeavour.

13

Master and learn the power of the principles of leverage
"Give me a lever long enough and a fulcrum on which to place it and I shall move the world."
Archimedes - Mathematician and inventor of ancient Greece, 280-211bc

Leverage is a very exceptional productivity enhancing technique that can be applied to any endeavour where we need to succeed. It simply asks the question:

"How can I increase my level of success, speed and time in the achievement of my objective?"

Hence there is the need for us to get intentional and strategic in the use of leverage in every part of our lives: personal and professional.

Leverage principle if understood can be applied literally into different things – thoughts and ideas, information or data as well as people.

For example you can expand your means by learning from other people's thoughts and ideas from books. Gain access to wide range of information from sourcing information from libraries and applying the information as new knowledge. Develop better understanding about yourself and hence giving you the ability to develop rapport in your relationship with people. You need the power of network of people because the value of a network has been is linked to the number of people in it. Your ability to master leverage is keen to your success in life.

Understanding leverage system

I read an interesting article on the power of leverage by Brad Gillies (bradgillies.com). In the article he reasoned that there are three parts to leverage.

The Dream

The Fulcrum

The lever itself

The Dream – This is the objective that you intend to bring into reality. The most successful individuals focus on a dream that advances humanity, it adds values. Therefore you need to ask the hard question: "What is the value or objective of my idea?"

The Fulcrum – This is the second part of the leverage system that you are building. It refers to YOU! You are the object upon which the lever pivots, without you there is no height t to the lever and the objective will never move no matter how much force is applied to the lever. Perhaps we need to borrow some inspirations here from the advice of Warren Hilton on resolve in attacking business problems is to have: the right mental attitude. You need to have the courage and confidence that what you are desiring to establish will succeed.

The lever itself – This is the third aspect of constructing the leverage system. When the objective and the fulcrum are in place, success depends **on the length and strength of the lever.** The two key words here: the length and the strength of the lever are important of note. It is important that the lever is strong and long for the following reasons:

The strength of the lever is important because less force will be required to move the object. Again a long lever works easier and faster than a short one.

Successful people understand that where performance in business is concerned speed is the new currency of business and therefore they create very long and very strong levers. The key idea here is to think about how to position yourself in your present environment so as to maximise your potential to serve as many people as possible.

Areas you can leverage for maximum impact for success in life and business

The key thing in business is to get things done with available resources. However because the resources are scarce it is our responsibility to see ways to add value to the resources and hence our outcome; which will result in greater effectiveness in the use of systems available to us so as to increase productivity. Leveraging is an important tool for expanding our means, reducing the time for the process as well as activities, leading to excellent results. Simply put, to do more with less!

The following are some of the strategies that you can use to leverage your outcome.

1. Time – leverage your time so that whatever work you perform today will pay you over and over again. This is my hope and faith in writing this book.

2. Other people's time – leverage other peoples time so that so that you can be paid on the efforts of other people. For example, starting you own business and employing others to work for you.

3. Your money – leverage your money so that your money works for you instead of you constantly having to work for your money. This is the key different between the rich and the poor. The works for their money and in turn make their money work for them through investing it in profitable business ventures. The poor blows away all they have and have nothing left. On the other hand the rich see the dollar they have as a seed for more dollars.

4. Other people's money – leverage other people's money, in other to generate income that you would otherwise have not this ability to generate.

5. Your own experience - You can leverage an experience you have in life - good or bad for common good. What have you learned from this experience? Who can benefit from it? How can I share it with others? There is power in asking and answering your own questions. The answer to the question may be the beginning of a book, workshop, seminar or the whole experience couls result in career change to public speaking.

6. Other people's experience - It takes too long to learn a new skill or craft so borrow or learn from others. This is in fact the basis for modelling other people's skill in NLP. Mastery of any body of knowledge requires continuous practice, action and review of your strategies. How long it takes depends on you. I want share with you the learning system adopted by Benjamin Franklin which led to his great success in different fields – writing, publishing, science, business and governance.

Step1 – Identify an expert who is already proficient in the skill you wish to acquire. This expert should be someone whose work you greatly admire and whose style or method you aspire to match.

Step 2 – Imitate the master you've identified in step 1. Do this by studying his or her work, directly or indirectly and internalizing that work in order get a true understanding and then reproduce the work on your own.

Step 3 – Practice imitating the work until you've achieved your own mastery of the desired skill.

He used this strategy to hone his writing and improve his influencing skill modelled according to The Spectator – a daily journal and Socrates –the great Greek philosopher.

You can really model any experience, For example, you can model a wealthy man to understand their source of great wealth. The easiest way is to apprentice with one who is wealthy or learn all you can about them and put their experience into practice. You can follow these people thanks to the power of the internet through Twitters, Facebook and U-tube. You can sign up to their newsletters so as to read their ideas and thoughts on their specialist subject. Read their books, listen to their audios, and attend their seminars or workshops. Do all you can do to keep abreast of the developments in your chosen expert/specialist knowledge but more than anything put what you've learnt into practice. What I have been sharing with you is based on these principles of learning from great minds.

Just one idea you learn can save you 10 years of hard work and effort.

Leverage is about maximizing your result in a minimum amount of time.

7. Other people's idea – you need to associate with other people who can show you the nut and bolts that nailed their success together. In terms of business success that will lead to great wealth the following strategies work.

- Find a mentor
- Develop a team
- Leverage network
- Leverage infinite networks
- Leverage tools and skills
- Leverage systems

Succeeding with people – develop great people's skill

The most important single ingredient in the formula of success knows how to get along with people.
- Theodore Roosevelt

At the beginning of this work I tried to explain the real meaning of success based on the definition by John Maxwell (see page 5). But to recount we reasoned that:

Success is to know your purpose in life, growing to reach your maximum potential, and sowing seeds that benefit others. Let us assume that you now have discovered your purpose, strived and is still making effort to reach your maximum potential, and you now want to sow seed that benefits others. Essentially, in sowing the seed that benefits others you have to serve people in one form or the other based on the idea, service, or product that you bring to the market place. How successful you become in this will be determined on how you are able to get along with people. Indeed Theodore Roosevelt is very correct.

Moreover, Zig Ziglar the expert on self-development had this to say:

"You can have everything you want in life if you help enough other people get what they want."

No wonder the part to greatness is to take the servant role; Christ like attitude.

What can you do with your talents, gifts, skills, specialist knowledge, and life's great experiences?

How can you expand your means by using it to serve many people? **This is the part to blessing.** Just begin within what you have and where you are. Do whatever you set your heart upon to do with the desire to serve. If you want great reward give a greater service.

Some people put money as their focus in their bid to services. However, money is the harvest of our production and service; which we use to obtain the production and service of others.

Wait for a moment and look through history. What is it that distinguished the great men and women who contributed and made a different in diverse fields of knowledge? They served many. Let's take for example Bill Gates – he brought computing into our homes and in the process served many and the reward was that he became very rich. Take another example. Henry Ford who made automobile accessible to the common man; he served many and became successful as a result. There are many other examples out there. One thing is common for these men, they hard a purpose, achieved their dreams and in their bid served many and were rewarded in the process. Their limited background was not an obstacle but they learned and forged on as they moved with laser focus and with great determination to their goals.

Listen to what Robert T Kiyosaki said in the book that he co-authored with Donald Trump – "Why we want you to be Rich"

"It is not the quest for money that makes me rich. It is the quest for knowledge. It is the desire to learn more, do more, accomplish more and help those who want to learn that drives me ... and money is just the score, a measure to tell me how we are doing."

W. J Cameron said that: "Money never starts an idea; it is the idea that starts the money."

What idea (s) do you have? Have you explore it or are you on the way towards exploring them? Are you on your success journey towards achieving your potential? Or if you have achieved your potential; what is your idea to serve others with your talent?

After all, according to Theodore Levitt - Professor of Marketing at Harvard; the purpose of a business is to create and serve a customer

I leave you with these pertinent questions:

"How do you create a customer? How do you keep a customer? How do you create more customers? You need to become a big picture thinker so as to expand your experience and also expand your world. This will help you to accomplish more than you were to remain narrow minded in your thinking. Become fluent in your thinking as you seek to embrace diverse dimensions – issues, people, relationships, timings and values. Learn and seek to understand other people's thinking habits as well what make them thick and seek ways to support or help them achieve their need or wants.

Above all - learn to sell
"Sales skill is the *dynamic* factor of success. It transforms potential powers into actual accomplishments. It enables the qualified man to turn his individual capabilities to best account."
Norvan A Hawkins – Author of Uncertain Success

In his book "Certain Success" by Norval, A Hawkins; he reasoned that for an individual to be successful in any market place the following principles must be understood and applied in your particular areas. It is made up of the following four vital steps:

(1) Knowing how to sell

(2) The true idea

(3) Of one's best capabilities

(4) In the right market or field of service.

Remembering that how successful you become in the marketplace is based on the values you add to it in terms of the results you bring. If you "have the goods" and would succeed certainly in your chosen vocation, you must sell to the world or to individual buyers true ideas about your particular qualifications for success--true ideas regarding your best capabilities and the value of your services. Your "goods of sale" may be your muscular power; your brain energy; your talents, skill, integrity, and knowledge in this capacity or in that. Whatever qualities you possess, it is necessary that someone be sold the idea of their full worth, or you cannot succeed. No matter how valuable your services might be, they have only potential worth until another man, or some business, or the world at large perceives desirable possibilities in you and buys the expectation that you will "deliver the goods." The secret of certain success in life for you, then, whatever your vocation or ambition, lies in knowing HOW to sell true ideas of your best capability in the right market or field of service. The golden chance is gained by another--less qualified and less worthy, perhaps; but *a better salesman of himself*. The fully competent man, however, can *assure* his success by becoming proficient in selling true ideas of his best capability in the right market or field of service. The master salesman of himself makes his own chances to succeed, and therefore runs no risk of being overlooked by Opportunity.

The opportunity to sell your merchandise is everywhere. Look all around your present environment. Opportunity is solution to an inconvenience. Opportunity is feeling. Opportunity is comfort. Opportunity is better service. Opportunity is fixing pain. Opportunity is putting poor performing businesses out of business. Opportunity is raising your potential and positioning yourself to a position of power to share in life's abundance.

Do you know the Law of income? "You will be paid in direct proportion to the **value** you deliver according to the marketplace" Pay close attention to the word value in this statement. There are four factors that determine value in the market place; these are: supply, demand, quality and quantity. The key factor that separates the successful and not so successful in any marketplace is quantity. I will ask you this question? What is the difference between small and big business? Simply, it is the number of customers that they serve. The quantity factor is how much of your value that you actually deliver in the marketplace.

. How can you create more value to your clients? How can you put a system in place in terms of plans, principles and procedures to serve more people? What specialist knowledge do you need to increase and improve your service?

Imagine your reward if you can serve more people in the marketplace by adding more value in any of the following areas of human need:

1. Make them feel better
2. Educate them
3. Make them look better (health, nutrition, clothing, beauty)
4. Give them security (housing, safety, health)
5. Raise a positive emotion (love, happiness, laughter,
6. Help them solve a problem
7. Satisfy appetites from basic food to life's pleasures.
8. Make things easier
9. Enhance their dreams and give hope

The more people you serve the more the value of your contribution and hence your reward. You need to work intelligently and see ways to serve more people in your chosen career or vocation. The more your contribution, the more you will be rewarded – in tangible and intangible ways.

I suggest that you increase your knowledge in business, psychology, sales and marketing. Find world leaders in these specialist fields and model how they do what they do.

Activity 13: **Master and learn the power of the principles of leverage**

1. In your personal and professional life think about the way that you can devise and use systems to improve your productivity – do more with less and with speed.

2. How can you develop the same concept in your business life in the way of the systems that you have put in place?

3. If you are working for yourself how can you reach more customers so as to serve more people and profit more,

4. How can the ideas in step 7 of page 74 be applicable to your services so as to improve your ability in what you do?

Conclusion

"Success is being on the road towards something we want to bring about."

Earl Nightingale – Author Lead the Field

The key point I want you to engrave into your mind is that achievement must have a cause. Accomplishments of any sort or form are not pulled out of the air; there is no place for chance. The laws and principles of God are not based on chance.

"Chance is a word of void sense and nothing can exist without a cause."

-Voltaire

Chance is of no effect, only choice will work.

On the whole the first step to be successful is the determination to succeed. Develop your thinking. Decide to achieve a purpose. Set goal and plans to direct you in the direction of your destination and hence your destiny. Take massive action but be flexible as to your result as your plan changes. You need to exercise patience, determination, persistence and courageousness. According to James Allen the author of "As a man thinketh"; there can be neither progress nor achievement without sacrifice and a man's worldly success will be by the measure that he sacrifices his confused animal thought and fixes his mind on the development of his plans, and the strengthening of his resolution and self-reliance. The higher he lifts his thoughts, the greater will be his success, the more blessed and enduring will be his achievement.

The journey to your goal results in your development of Mastery. You become a bigger person. You have new skills, new attitudes and new capabilities.

Writing this book has been a journey for me and it has also changed my perspectives in terms of the new possibilities as to what is possible. My desire was to find a way to organise what I learned from diverse thought leaders in this field of raising human potential. This opportunity to share it in this book with you the reader is a thing of joy.

I leave you with this quote from Earl Prevette on the attitude of success:

"Get the attitude of success, think and feel it. A flower girl of London looked like a duchess, thought like a duchess, talked like a duchess, acted like a duchess and soon become a duchess in the play 'Pygmalion'"

Above all things have implicit faith in God's providence; He alone will make your desires come true.

"Commit thy work unto the Lord, and thy thought s shall be established."

- **Psalm 26:2**

SUCCESS QUOTES

Don't aim for success if you want it; just do what you love and believe in, and it will come naturally. [*David Frost*]

Always bear in mind that your own resolution to succeed is more important than any other. [Abraham Lincoln]

Defeat is not the worst of failures. Not to have tried is the true failure. [George Edward Woodberry]

Develop success from failures. Discouragement and failure are two of the surest stepping stones to success. [Dale Camegie]

Don't confuse fame with success. Madonna is one; **Helen Keller** is the other. [Erma Bombeck]

Flaming enthusiasm, backed up by horse sense and persistence, is the quality that most frequently makes for success. [Dale Carmegle]

Formula for success: rise early, work hard, strike oil. [J. **Paul Getty**]

How can they say my life is not a success? Have I not for more than sixty years got enough to eat and escaped being eaten? [Logan P. Smith]

I couldn't wait for success, so I went ahead without it. [**Jonathan Winters**]

I don't know the key to success, but the key to failure is trying to please everybody. [Bill Cosby]

I honestly think it is better to be a failure at something you love than to be a success at something you hate. [George Burns]

I've failed over and over and over again in my life and that is why I succeed. [Michael Jordan]

If at first you don't succeed, try, try again. Then quit. There's no point in being a damn fool about it. [W.C. Fields]

If you want to achieve things in life, you've just got to do them, and if you're talented and smart, you'll succeed. [Juliana Hatfield]

In order to succeed you must fail, so that you know what not to do the next time. [Anthony J. D'Angelo]

In order to succeed, your desire for success should be greater than your fear of failure. [Bill Cosby]

Pray that success will not come any faster than you are able to endure it. [Elbert Hubbard]

Success consists of going from failure to failure without loss of enthusiasm. [Winston Churchill]

Success in almost any field depends more on energy and drive than it does on intelligence. This explains why we have so many stupid leaders. [Sloan Wilson]

Success is blocked by concentrating on it and planning for it... Success is shy - it won't come out while you're watching. [Tennessee Williams]

Success is how high you bounce when you hit bottom. [George S. Patton]

Success is often the result of taking a misstep in the right direction. [Al Bernstein]

Success is simply a matter of luck. Ask any failure. [Earl Wilson]

Success is to be measured not so much by the position that one has reached in life as by the obstacles which he has overcome. [Booker T. Washington]

Success isn't a result of spontaneous combustion. You must set yourself on fire. [Arnold H. Glasow]

Success seems to be largely a matter of hanging on after others have let go. [William Feather]

Success without honour is an unseasoned dish; it will satisfy your hunger, but it won't taste good. [Joe Patemo]

The ladder of success is best climbed by stepping on the rungs of opportunity. [Ayn Rand]

The man who has done his level best... is a success, even though the world may write him down a failure. [B.C. Forbes]

The measure of success is not whether you have a tough problem to deal with, but whether it is the same problem you had last year. [John Foster Dulles]

The most important single ingredient in the formula of success is knowing how to get along with people. [**Theodore Roosevelt**]

Try not to become a man of success, but rather try to become a man of value. [Albert Einstein]

Success is not the key to happiness. Happiness is the key to success. If you love what you are doing, you will be successful. - Albert Schweitzer

There is nothing as useless as doing efficiently that which should not be done at all. - Peter Drucker

The secret of success is constancy to purpose. - Benjamin Disraeli

It's not what we don't know that prevents us from succeeding; it's what we know that just ain't so that is our greatest obstacle – Josh Billings

About the Author

Benjamin is an avid reader, long life learner in the field of personal development as well as a writer. He writes in the Hubpages.com and you can read his articles at:

http://lemmyc.hubpages.com/

He has also has written a book titled: Progress Path: Discover innovative ideas on how to make progress in life and work. The book can be accessed through this link: http://www.lulu.com/content/e-book/progress-path-discover-innovative-ideas-on-how-to-make-progress-in-life-and-work/9364048

He is the Founder of Progress Path – Mastery Education a learning organisation dedicated to enabling people, grow and contribute to the society through teaching specialist knowledge.

He has his background in science and education and has motivated himself to acquire special knowledge in the fields of management, psychology as well as sales and marketing. His passion is to enable people realise their potential and this is the motivation for putting this work together.

He was a Rotary Ambassadorial Scholar and British Council Study Fellow; and an alumnus of University of Leeds and Leeds Metropolitan University both in the United Kingdom. He has a Certificate in Personal Coaching from the Coaching Academy, UK.

Ben is a born again Christian and worships at Bridge Street Pentecostal Church in Leeds; where he lives; and is happily married with three children.

www.ingramcontent.com/pod-product-compliance
Lightning Source LLC
Chambersburg PA
CBHW070432290526
45791CB00005B/1944